"Jenna's Brother Has Autism"

Written and Illustrated by,

Amber L. Fernbach

"Jenna's Brother Has Autism",

This book is dedicated to my children, the loves of my life, Joshua and Jessica.

I give all glory to God for giving me my children, my husband Mike, my family, and all the therapists, teachers, and workers that He has put into our path to help us along the journey of living with autism.

Jenna's Brother Has Autism

"Attention students, will everyone please look up here?" "Jenna wants you all to meet her brother, Jonathan", says Mrs. Meyers, "Jonathan is autistic." The students sat attentively in their seats and gave their attention to Jenna. "Hi everybody", Jenna said, "this is my brother, Jonathan; he has autism." The kids continued to look at Mrs. Meyers and Jenna. They all wanted to hear what Jenna had to say about her brother, Jonathan.

Mrs. Meyers asked the children to say "hi" to Jonathan. They all waved and sang out, "Hi Jonathan." Jonathan's body tensed with excitement. He smiled awkwardly and waves and yells, "hi". Mrs. Meyers turned to the classroom and said, "Ok class, we're going to have a time where you all can ask Jenna questions so that you can learn a bit about what it is like to live with autism.

Mary raised her hand and asked, "How old are you, Jonathan?" Jonathan jumped up and down and yelled "six"! Mrs. Meyers explained, "Jonathan is so excited to be here and see all you children." Jonathan is so happy, but he doesn't quite know how to express himself. It is as if he is bursting with happiness!

Jacob raised his hand, and asked, "What *is* autism?" "There is a set of behaviors that determine whether or not a person can be labeled 'autistic'." It has a lot to do with understanding others." "Some autistic children have trouble using their imagination and playing." "Other autistic people may not talk or show much interest in others at all." "Like a rainbow has many colors, autism has many variations… or degrees." "Autism is a 'spectrum' of which there are many forms; some people show a lot of traits, or symptoms, and others, exhibit, or show very little." "Jonathan is somewhere in the middle."

Megan asked, "Can his doctor give him medicine? "Mrs. Meyers said, "He has a special doctor, called a 'developmental pediatrician' who helps Jonathan get set up for therapies.

After raising his hand, Jacob asked, "Will he get better?" Jenna and Mrs. Meyers both smile. Mrs. Meyers replies, "Well, autism isn't something that just *goes* away; Jonathan will need lots of teaching and therapy along the way." "With teaching and therapy, some symptoms may fade."

Meanwhile, Jonathan had gotten bored while standing in front of the class. He wandered over to the play area and began to play with a train set – one of his favorite types of toys!

Jenna looked towards her brother, and explained to the class that Jonathan has a limited attention span. "If he's interested, he can pay attention for a while, if not, he easily gets distracted."

"What kind of teaching, or therapies?", questioned Mary. "Jonathan started with speech therapy" said Jenna. "He does work at home, too", she added. "Yes," said Mrs. Meyers, "he does strict therapy at home as well." His therapy began as teaching him to follow simple directions, like, "come here", and got more difficult as he mastered every task." "Therapists go into their home every day of the week and work with him for a couple hours at a time", said Jenna. "He also goes to an *autistic support* kindergarten class", states Jenna.

"Why does he grunt, and flap his arms?" questioned Gracie. "Well, that's called 'stimming'," explained Mrs. Meyers. "He does that to release a type of energy or emotion." "To him, it's a normal action which he does not know how to hold back." "Some autistic people do this a lot; some hardly do it at all."

Lindsay asked, "Does Jonathan have ADHD like *my* brother?" Mrs. Meyers said, "No, Jonathan does not have ADHD; although autism may sometimes seem similar." "With ADHD, people have trouble paying attention and are usually very active". "Autism can cause problems with attention, often due to not understanding". "But, with autism, there are other problems that people with ADHD do not usually have." "Like, not liking certain foods because of the way they feel in your mouth. Or, seeing the brightness of lights and being upset

because they're too bright, or making a humming noise. People with autism are often sensitive to sounds, and activities going on around them. It is as if they notice *everything* all at once, and have trouble taking it all in, processing it in their brains."

Caden raised his hand, "Is Jonathan always so happy?" Jenna giggled as she answered, "No, he isn't always so happy." "He often gets very frustrated. If things do not go *his* way, or if they go differently than *he* expects, he is so easily upset. He also gets confused if his routine is changed and he doesn't understand why." "If my mom tells him 'no'," Jessica added, "he doesn't always understand or accept an explanation."

"What is life like at home?" asked Cody? "Well", Jenna said, "it is a little different." Jonathan is not so severe." "Sometimes his lack of understanding is frustrating, but overall, it's really good." Jonathan plays with me, and rides his Big Wheel; we jump on the trampoline together. Jonathan *loves* to jump!" "He also loves to wrestle with our dad and plays video games with him too." "There is a lot of physical play, but not too much with imagination. Jonathan helps out, and loves to hear, 'good job!'. Jonathan loves kisses from my mom, and he gives great hugs."

Ally raised her hand and asked, "What is the most difficult thing with having an autistic brother?" "Hmmm…." Said Jenna, "I guess when Jonathan doesn't understand certain things that are said or done. He can get easily frustrated and will cry and scream; it is a tantrum. He is difficult to calm down sometimes."

 "What can we do to help other autistic people and children?", asked Kaylee. Mrs. Meyers replied, "Patience and understanding." "The best thing we can do is be patient, understand, and try to listen to autistic people and their needs and feelings. Try to put yourself in their shoes; see what may be upsetting them. Try to understand how it's frustrating when you, yourself are misunderstood."

"Well, children," said Mrs. Meyers, "it's almost lunch time, and Jonathan needs to get back to his class." "Let's all thank Jonathan for coming to visit us." "Thaaaank you Jonathan!" the class sang out. Jonathan jumped up and down, once again, excited to be there. "You're welcome!" he said.

A Note About the Author:

My name is Amber Smerdon Fernbach and I am the mother of two children with "special needs". My children are Joshua and Jessica. However, Joshua is almost 12 years old and Jessica is 10 years old. Joshua's autism is mild, but mostly stereotypic. Jessica was diagnosed with PDD NOS (Pervasive Developmental Disorder, Not Otherwise Specified). Basically, her main delay was speech; she didn't talk until she was 4 years old!

My husband, Mike, and I both went to school for *applied behavioral science* at Pennsylvania State University (PSU). I credit our schooling to noticing small abnormalities in Joshua's and Jessica's development. Seeing these, we were able to begin the children with services in early intervention.

Having children with these problems is difficult. There are a lot of people who do not understand autism and its traits (symptoms). Some people have no knowledge (or education) about autism, PDD, ADD, or ADHD. Thankfully, we live in a time where there is much research that has been done on autism, and much work still being done. Children and people with these problems have more access to help than was available even 10-15 years ago.

For years, I have wondered why my children were born like this. I do not have an answer. But, I think, maybe God wanted me to try and help others in similar situations understand, and help them find answers, and ways to help their children.

Education and awareness are VERY important.

I know the number of cases of diagnosed autism are on the rise. I want to help others understand. I wrote this book on a child's level, hoping it can help classmates, siblings, and friends to better understand autism.

This book is not only limited to children. It is also for adults out there who may not know a lot about autism. It is to meant to give awareness to autism so that people can be empowered by the knowledge they have.

This is my first book and I want to thank you for reading. I hope I have the opportunity to write more for the cause of autism and similar disorders.

www.ingramcontent.com/pod-product-compliance
Lightning Source LLC
Chambersburg PA
CBHW041233040426
42444CB00002B/146